T0171371

The Genesis

The Genesis

A COLLECTION OF POEMS

Mekael

Copyright © 2007 by Mekael.

ISBN: Hardcover   978-1-4257-6628-3
                 Softcover   978-1-4257-6626-9

All rights reserved. No part of this book may be reproduced or transmitted in any form or by any means, electronic or mechanical, including photocopying, recording, or by any information storage and retrieval system, without permission in writing from the copyright owner.

This book was printed in the United States of America.

To order additional copies of this book, contact:
Xlibris Corporation
1-888-795-4274
www.Xlibris.com
Orders@Xlibris.com
38886

Contents

THE REBELLION

PROLOGUE

THE REFLECTION

PROLOGUE

THE REDEMPTION

PROLOGUE

This collection is dedicated to

My mother

Joyce L. Maul

November 1951 to March 2006

About the Author

Mekael L. Shane was born in Indianapolis, Indiana, on October 17th, 1970. He is his mother's middle child, and he says that he strongly believes in the complexities and uniqueness that comes from being *"the middle"* child. He developed a love for writing early in his life, and always thought that he would have a career in writing. He attributes his love for all things literary to his high school literature teachers and his college professors, but, he says that his foundational source of exposure to literature was birthed from his mother. While working to earn her degree in Journalism, she would often ask Mekael to proof read her work, to write something comparative to her work, and to edit her work. This of course had a powerful affect on his love of all things technical involved with writing.

Mekael says devoutly, *"My high school literature teacher, Mr. Foxlow impressed upon me, a love for the traditionalist, the transcendentalist, the romance authors and especially the authors of the Harlem Renaissance period. Mr. Foxlow was of course impassioned about the likes of Yeats, Thoreau, Rimbaud, Shakespere and Emerson especially since he was from England".* Mekael says that this love became more expounded when he went away to college. He says that it was while there at Central State University of Ohio that his love for the written arts deepened. He says that it was there that he was allowed to grasp a stronger, more in depth appreciation for African American Authors and Poets.

A product of his generation, the hip-hop generation, Mekael speaks of today's hip-hop Poets with the same admiration that he has for the Renaissance Poets and the rest of today's contemporary Poetic vanguard. He believes that the stellar Hip-Hop Poets of today like Mos Def, Common, Nas, Tupac, Biggie, Eminem, and Jay-Z are reflective of the continued presence of their Poetic forefathers and foremothers. Mekael believes that we will be impacted by the spirits of, Langston Hughes, Paul Laurence Dunbar, Zora Hurston, Dr. Maya Angelou, Mari Evans, Nikki Giovanni, Amiri Barraka, The Lost Poets, Ntozake Shange, Gil Scot-Heron, Asha Bandele and the countless others who have held the torch high. Mekael believes that it's time for the new generation of the vanguard to stand up and to heed the call, accepting the mantle with both pride and courage.

Mekael states emphatically that he prays that his writing will one day, positively affect the lives of young people fostering in them, an affinity for the written arts. Mekael states, *"I pray that my Poetry touches the life of just one person. I pray that it affects this person's life in a way that promotes positivity and empowerment. It was during the creation of this collection that I was made to see myself, and I cannot speak enough of how hard it is to be made to see "yourself". To be made to look deep inside of your being and to circumspect about your life and your journey. This wasn't an easy task, but, I know that to become the man that God ordained me to be, I must assess me in order to get to the better me that He designed me to be. I think that this collection does a great job at detailing who I was, who I am, and who I am to become. I hope that this collection generates dialog, and thought. I hope that it challenges some, while it helps to change others. Ultimately, I pray, that all who read it, simply enjoy it."*

Acknowledgements

First and foremost, I must with total humility, acknowledge the presence and the power of God. I know beyond any inference of doubt, that He has blessed me. He has been the bedrock of my strength and I acknowledge that I am truly blessed because of the incredible favor that He has shown me, my whole life long. It was during a moment of intense tribulation in my life that I sought counsel with my uncle, who is also one of my spiritual guides, the Reverend, Dr. Preston T. Adams. I went to him seeking an answer to a question that was crippling me spiritually. My question was, *"why me?"* His answer was, *"why not you?"* He then decided to delve deeper into why answering my original question, with a question was so important. What he said will stay with me forever *"You must learn your purpose in life, then you must make a statement of desiring God's allowance for you to become what He has destined for you to become. Once you have done that, then you must work to sow the seeds of understanding, in what it is that He means for your life's purpose to be. Then and only then, will God know through your actions, and your heart, that you are deserving of all of the gifts that He has waiting for you."* Since that conversation, I have prayed that God sees my desire and that He knows my heart.

As I worked to bring this project to a close, and as I readied it and prepared it for production, I was consumed with thoughts of my mother, Joyce Maul. She has and always will be for me, a source of fuel to my heart's fire. She was there with me from the beginning, when I wrote my first poem ten years ago, and though she has been removed from the world physically, she still sits beside me, in her oversight over my ultimate project, my life. There's not a day that passes that I don't hear her laughter, or that I don't hear her pushing me to, *"write, write, write!"* which were her immortal words of inspiration to me. I miss you Ma, and we made it.

I want to acknowledge the role that my family, the Mauls, have played in my life. You all have been pillars of strength and wisdom for me and I am eternally thankful to you for all of your support and guidance. You have no idea what you mean to me.

I must also acknowledge my siblings, Marcellus and Rhonda. We promised each other that we'd insure that we would reach those better days together. You two have been a constant source of motivation for me. Thank you.

To my *"crew"* of friends, Kevin Stone, Terris Radcliff, Mychal Wharton and Vontres Brents, I lined you all up by height, not by order of importance, for you all are of equal importance to my life. You men have always supported me and have kept me motivated, especially during some of the most hellish moments in my life. I am blessed to have you all as brothers.

To the brothers in my fraternity, the men who meet me on the *"level"*, my coaches and my many mentors, I say thank you. You have helped to mold and shape me, forging me through fire into a man of standard and strength. You challenged me to step toward greatness and this project is my salute to you.

To the many editors, proof readers, and my production team at Xlibris, especially Noel Flowers and Jerry Coville, I say thank you for supporting me and my vision, helping to turn a dream into reality. I am eternally grateful.

Genesis—"The origination, commencement, or the beginning of Creation, Life, or Human existence
Human Rebellion
And
Restoration through the promise of Redemption"

Prologue ... The Rebellion

Many of the Poems in this section of my collection are expressive of what my opinion was concerning the world around me when I was about twenty-five or twenty-six years old. Life in my home city had become truly rowdy and extremely rough, due to the heightened level of the rushed inflow of drugs which led to a series of killings during that year which of course went unsolved and unattended to. That year, 1996, was wrought with the loss of so many of my friends and peers that I began to feel disenfranchised and disconnected from my community. I was utterly confused and I felt that things could only get better through prayer, and some ground pounding. I remember how while praying during that time, that I would ask God to show me what it was that I could do to help affect change in my city.

I remember how I would wake up and find that I ultimately wasn't able to find any peace in my sleep during those days. I remember thinking that, stakes were high and things had become so drastic that, I might end up losing quite a few friends from my old neighborhood, that there wouldn't be too many of us left. Well, I was right. I now walk those streets, in the hopes of reminiscing about my days as a child and my early teenage years. Those were the most unsullied and most innocuous years of my life. Now when I walk those streets, I may see a ghostly figure, that used to be a childhood friend, but who was now a zombie like fiend because of crack cocaine. Crack, the most horrific of all insidious pandemics, that our communities and cities nationwide, are still feeling the affects of the genesis of crack. I was also losing many of my friends because of the crack monster, and I knew that I would have to create a plan, to help fight the crack demon.

I figured that if I could write about the strife and stress that was driving the communities in my city toward destruction, then I would be doing my part to help change the explosive environment that I was existing in at that time. I then became so prolific in my creating Poetry that year, that I felt like my mind and my fingers were going to burst from everything that was building up. In my mind, I had so many things to say and I remember that I needed to figure out how to best, format every single thought into a Poetic form of expression. My fingers were going to burst because of all of the typing that I was doing during that oh so hectic period.

I remember how after going from one funeral, to the next funeral, and then onto the next funeral, I kept saying to myself, *"I had better get out there and start spreading the words of peace and rejuvenation to my people"*. This belief is what drove me to attend my very first open-mic Poetry reading. I had four pieces of Poetry with me, and they were all filled with the kind of subject matter that focused on the volatility that was occurring daily.

That very first Poetry reading had such a profound affect on me that I started to network to find out when more Poetry readings were scheduled to happen, so that I could attach myself to them. Again, this was my own little form of resistance and rebellion toward all of the violence that was taking place and I knew that if I could reach just one listener, if I could reach just one young person and make him see that things didn't have to remain like they were, then I would be victorious.

It was during one city-wide Black History Month celebratory event that was to take place that I was invited to participate in, that I knew I was on the right track. That particular Poetry event was not only a celebration of Black History Month, but it was to also celebrate an amazing Poet, who had passed a few years earlier, the great Etheridge Knight, whom that Poetry reading was named after was a great gathering place for local Poets in the city of Indianapolis. It was while there at the celebration, that I saw the amazing affect that Poetry can have on people, though, I already knew the affect that it had on me. But it was after I read a Poem titled 'Guterborne Hero' that a teenage boy walked up to me and said something that has stayed with me, ever since he uttered those words. He said, *"I now know what I want to be, I want to be a Poet, just like you"*. After hearing this teenager say that to me, I went home and sat there on the couch and just pondered deeply, unto myself.

That night, my mom, who had been at the Poetry reading, came over to visit with me for a while, and as usual she began to talk about some of her life's experiences. She specifically liked to share with me how she had been at a reading in Chicago and had seen Haki Madhubuti live and heard him recite one of his most prophetic Poems, *'Black Christ'*, I believe was the title she spoke of. She said that it was that Poem that made her fall in love with Poetry, along with Langston Hughes' most awe inspiring Poetic creation, *'Mother to Son'*. After listening to my mom and her verboseness, I had to tell her about this young boy and I had to tell her how this boy's words were powerful and that I felt that they would have an affect on me, long past that night. I told her that, I felt that it was in that moment, that it wasn't this teenage speaking to me, but that rather, it was God. I felt that it was God saying to me, *"You will from this moment on, be a role model, whether you want to or not"*. I remember telling my mother that, I felt as though I had to accept and heed that call to arms, so to speak, and that I needed to start operating with an air of distinction in everything that I did, especially since, a person never knows who might be watching them, learning from them, and how whatever it is that some person sees us do, that we could be either confirming a spirit or a thought of negativity, or we could be planting a seed of positivity. I am ever so thankful to that teenager for being the conduit for which God made use of to send me a very powerful message.

The Rebellion

Absolution

Pseudo are those around me, by their pheromones alone I sense their trepidation
Truth ensnared by rage, moments of reflection enslave their conscience
As the look of cowardice fills their eyes, I again can smell their hesitation
As I greet one, he smiles as he claims to wish me well
While deep inside the cacophony like pit of his soul, I know he wishes me hell
His contradicting smile tells the truth of this story
Not bound by symbolisms, not made farcical by any allegory

It's not that they envy what I don't own, for I possess no material wealth
It's that they wish to find the source of my strength; the gift is my spiritual health
I have accepted these trappings, and have laid waste to so many burnt bridges
Which were innocently set ablaze, by the pyromaniacal days of my youthful living
They have thought to study my secrets, trying to figure out my pathology
The proof is in my roots, and for that I make no apology
Born a hellish corrupted seed, because of my father's dirty deeds
I claim no victimization, because of mine own reckless pursuits
Finding closure is now my quest, for its truth is so absolute

Along The Halls

Wrist clamped together
Shackles connecting your hands and feet
You are allowed to take only baby steps
All the while, the steel feast on your flesh
As if it were cheap petty meat
You are caught up by the dope that you cooked
And here you are isolated
Surrounded by many but yet and still you are alone
Left to survive the gladiator filled nights
While in this encaged battle zone
Your enslaved history is forever recorded
In the penile institution's history books

As the Corrections Officer guides you along the halls
The stench in the air is reminiscent of death you think
You begin to feel haunted because you hear their hallowed calls
Shadows cast ghostly figures, leaving you pleading to be free
Then the cold grip of jailhouse reality snatches you up
Because of the mangled spirits and the terror that you see

You know instinctively that it will take more than man
To bring you through this journey unscathed
You reminisce for a moment thinking of the
Cesspool of ugly, in which you once knowingly bathed
You started out wanting to hustle
Because you were driven by your desire
To escape the poverty in which you were born
You are forced to decide between
Struggling to live free, or to die while on the grind
And this decision had you feeling torn
Your brethren may never understand
That you are a victim to all of nothing
Fooled by the things created by man

Andrew's Atonement

At seventeen he was labeled an outlaw by our litigious society
He then became a study subject for the criminal scholars
Forced to face days of both fear and anxiety
His crime was that, he put a bullet in the head of the man
That raped and killed his mother
He found himself alone in the world, left to fend for his autistic brother
Andrew was his birth name, but convict was the other
He would grow, maturing while gaining wisdom from his penile education
The courts were unforgiving, death row was his final destination
His date with fate would be December 26th, 1987
Andrew believed in God, but he worried that because he was a murderer
He'd be denied entry into Heaven
After years of fighting the courts, his last day quickly approached
His character wasn't pristine, his legacy wasn't above reproach
At times, he'd sit in the dark circumspecting about the night he landed in jail
He thinks to himself, *"As I entered these prison walls back then,*
I believed that I had walked through the gates of hell"
It was two hours before his time, no more having to live like a savage just to survive
He decided to meet with the Chaplain to purge his soul
Now that his last day had arrived

He remarked about how he couldn't believe that 28 years seemed to quickly pass
Tears swelled in his eyes, knowing the meal that he'd just eaten would be his last
The barber had sheared his hair down close on both his left leg and his head
He asked the Chaplain with innocence, what they would do with the body
After he was pronounced dead
The Chaplain claimed that he'd be buried proper, in an unmarked grave
"How sad" Andrew thought, no grave to mark his days
"Dead man walking!" the shout came, and Andrew stood up wide awake
He thought about his life, and the moment of that fatal mistake

As he walked in near slow motion down the last mile
He heard the voice of God, and he began to crack a smile
But it was in his last words that he sought absolution, as he said his last prayer
His last words were to God, and Andrew became oblivious to the onlooker's stares
There were no rescuing calls from the Governor
Declaring a stay of execution at the last moment
A sudden power surged signaled his life's end
But the true beginning of Andrew's atonement

A Drug Dealer Speaks

When you look at me, I want you to know who I am
You need to know my story, where I'm coming from and where I've been
In this world where all has the capacity to be crumbled
I will find foundation in the fact, that I know that I have been humbled
Though I am young, I have seen God's forgiving face
And I have felt His presence while along this walk
It's the fruits of Heaven that I know that I'll one day taste
Though some things aren't really what they seem
I have climbed the rungs of Jacob's ladder
In the dark cold of night, guided by my nightmarish dreams

I've walked next to scholars, and I have shaken hands with dope dealers
I've seen the serpent's soul, in the eyes of pseudo faith healers
I've dealt death to the unborn babies ´
Whose mothers I victimized by my crack cocaine
I've slaughtered the lamb of innocence
While doing the work of he who has no name

My deed was not committed because I desired notoriety or fame
I did it for the love of mammon, because of my lust for material things
I care not that I was the crusher of so many people's dreams
I only lived to sell that powder, to the zombie like dope fiends
So, don't act like you can't see me, or like you don't know me
I was taught the rules of this devilish game
Because it was many of you who showed me

Believe Me

I watch as young brothers hustle on the corners questing for life's best
They grow wild with courage
While hiding their deep set fears underneath their padded chest
Inflated due to the concealment of
An inferior model of a bulletproof vest
But if it's man made, you can't count on that vest being a sure bet
Believe me when I say, that their days are long and their nights are wild
They used to drive the old beat up clunkers
But now it's the brand new Mercedes that they profile

Carnal recklessness has led to them fathering a child on all sides of the city
The truth lies in their roots, their hearts knows no pity
Strapped with illegal steel, ready to expire another on a whim
Shots ring out loud, and another black male is lost, a wasted gem
Destruction in continuum adds to the confusion
They don't recognize that it's ultimately the devil that's using them
I'm speaking of this ultimate evil, this is all part of Satan's plan
Not a genocide directed by others, we can't continue to blame the white man
So believe me when I say, that there is a heavy price to be free
I bet that our forefathers never dreamed
That in this condition is where our people would be

Big Black Boots

From the days that I was tall enough to reach your knees
I was destined to be great; this is what you schooled me to believe
No dream was too high, no goal too much to achieve
For me to conquer the mountain, a plan would have to be conceived

I've lost three of my friends to needless violent deaths this year
And to lose another or my brother, is my worst most dreadful fear
I've continued to wipe away those innocence filled tears
Because of the loss of my friends, my victimized peers
There aren't many of us left, from the old neighborhood
What will become of our legacy?
What was that thing for which we stood?
So, for now I'll keep on stepping
Striving to be the best man that I can be because of my roots
No matter how hard the road
I'll keep on stomping in my big black boots

Bound and Lost

Can you hear the clamor filled cries of our ancestors?
Swallowed into the belly of those menacing slave dungeons
Their flesh becoming meshed into one with those locks and chains
Their bones and detritus aren't the only proof of their passing
I hear their bellowed calls beyond the remains
No faces, no traces, no drops of their precious blood on the stones
The walls of those vicious cacophonies captured their haunting moans

You must look beyond what's supposed to be their obvious remains
You must feel it deep inside your marrow, that's the resting place of their pain
There were so many stolen black babies
Snatched from within their mother's wombs
Little fragile lives thrown devilishly into the blaze
Ghostly visions of the innocent cast into a fiery tomb
Can you hear the clamor filled cries of our ancestors?
Encapsulated pain encased their horror and rage
Auctioned off like wild beasts, victims to slavery's unyielding cage
There they sat naked, bound and lost
Lost to slavery's oppressive grip, lost to slavery's cold dark maze

But Still

You have judged me to the fullest expanse of any judgmental possibility
But who stands in judgment of you, whilst you judge me?
Look deep into the truths of your own life's tale
Then you'll see that the foundation of your judicious processing
Is full of cracks, its brittle, its frail
You have clad me in a suit of clandestine armor
For in your mind, it's me that you set sail to fail
You desire not to see me succeed
Because in your heart, I was due to bear the cross to which I'm nailed

It may be hard for you to imagine me
Becoming the man that God destined me to be, both great and strong
You've cast me out to the wilds, and that mile is treacherous and long
It frightens you to envision me rising out of the ashen detritus and remains
I spread my wings as I take flight like the Phoenix
I have broken lose from the snares and chains
But yet and still you exile me to the isle of obscurity
When I am but an Eagle, who desires to fly free
Yet no matter how high I fly, still you'll judge me

Caine's Confusion

He was born of the Earth's most unbridled rage
He captivates his victims, while they exist in a somniferous daze
As a result of his power, babies are being born set sail to fail
Men of once Herculean strength are reduced to skeletons
Then are blown about by the slightest gale
He leaves your mind a mix of forgotten memories
Caine forces you to forget the days of your own life's tale

For him, you'll sell ounces of your soul
With each prolonged inhalation of his smoky death
You are beamed onto a star ship headed for Hades
Your boarding pass lies within each caustic breath
You were once an overachiever, educated with the elite
Now you are drawn from reality by Caine's deadly ambrosia
You claim that Caine's aftertaste is so sugary sweet
You pawn your sex for a crumb of Caine
As if it were petty goods or cheap rotten meat
You possess no Earthly wealth
You walk the devil's domain with no shoes on your feet

Have we allowed a generation to be massacred by this weightless shackle
As it pumps expeditiously through their veins
Have we forgotten that we must stand and fight the destructive power
Of la coca, also known as cocaine by name
We have seen enough of the apocalyptic affects of Hell's rawest fusion
We have been driven to the realm of paludal madness
So chaotically guided by Caine's confusion

Dictation from the Jungle

I see myself stepping through the jungle, along the concrete sidewalk
My spirit becomes immersed, full of the panther on the stalk
I grew up wild as a child, like an inquisitive panther cub
My mind was a lump of virgin clay
Developed by the ghetto's magical mud

I prowled through the inner city slums; I was like a beast, a predator male
I learned to identify danger, by its scent, its aroma, its smell
I grew wise to the secrets of camouflage and I've chased my prey until it fell
I was born into a lineage of savages; my paw prints will tell my tale

All the while, I've been pursued by the hunter in white
But he lacks the skills to capture me, so he is best defined as a catamite
He has plans to place me on exhibit, and afterward he'll lock me away in a cage
He wants to study my celestial mysteries
While I'm locked up because of my rage

So until I'm caught, I'll remain a creature of habit
Here to chase the success filled rabbit
I'll never be a beast that's humble
My senses have grown into an intense bundle
Because of the messages sent to me
This dictation from the jungle

Gotta Make a Million

As I sit in circumspect, thinking of the days when
We made sandwiches out of syrup and bread
Living in a broken down tenement
Forced to drink water filled with deadly lead
I remember the days of having no shoes my feet
Mama had it rough, and we barely if ever had meat to eat
But through all of those trials
We learned to be strong, gaining the skills necessary to compete
Whether it was on a field of strife, or super achieving in the classroom
Doubt was never present, neither was the dark cloud of gloom
My quest is infinite, my destination is sugar hill
Gotta do whatever it takes, my vision is as sharp as steel
I know that I have to pound the pavement until there's blood on my feet
Conquering all mountains is the mission, no matter how steep
My goal now is to work to save our children
And to give them the resources to win, I gotta make a million

Greater Than Gold

Take a second to look black man, look closely at your skin tone
You'll see that it possesses a magic, that's uniquely all its own
Like when the sun is totally unbearable and at it's strongest
It's because of the gift in your skin, that you can stay outside the longest
Take a second to look black man, look at the number of hues that it comes in
So what is that which is greater than gold? The answer is simple, your skin

Guided By No Maxims

Inner city soldiers are molded, but guided by no maxims
For most of their models are pimps and dope peddlers
Scarce are suitable mentors and
Rare is that biological father, who steps to the forefront
To help shape these incredibly precious minds
They will need a major miracle
A sweeping wind of change, from the most high
They face an unrelenting cycle of mental and spiritual defamation
It's Heaven or hell for these young black males
Deliverance from this paludal situation

Some are lost forever to the streets, forgotten is the gift of education
Either a cell or a grave, is their ultimate destination
What can you tell a 14 year old boy who's stuck selling crack
When he's the only bread winner in his family, providing all that they lack
It's been nearly 200 years since that day of grace called emancipation
Yet and still we are the lost souls, in this the most free of all nations
Inner city soldiers are guided by no maxims
Though they desire to see the wind of change
Tomorrow is a dream, and reality is their pain

Gutterborne Hero

Growing up wild in the hood, you had to be the first to blast
I prayed to make it out of the ghetto
But being young and black was such a tedious task
I became a thug monster, feared by the elderly
And a gutterborne hero to the neighborhood youth
I had rolls of blood money in my pockets
I thought that I was living large and trunk jewelry was my proof
So many sleepless nights, from the nightmarish visions
Of those whom I lost to bullets and blades
I saw Pimps beating their hoes
Bruises and black eyes hidden, cloaked under cheap shades
My spirit was engulfed, made flammable because of my hate and rage
I learned to hide from my reality, in a liquor filled haze
Those were times of deep seeded sorrow, swollen sullen days
I thought that a bright future didn't exist for me
Expired and incinerated, in a fiery blaze
A victim to all of nothing, left alone to journey the maze
An endless cycle of prolific moroseness, a never ending phase
Yeah there I was, I amounted to nothing even less than zero
Living a façadical existence, as a gutterborne hero

If You Could Only See

If you could only see, my desire for no nightmares is where I wish to be
Ghetto madness is only increasing
While the numbers of free black brothers, is slowly decreasing
It's either the round ball, or that deadly dope game
A fresh new raw talent, or that new jack searching for street fame
While my people continue to suffer
Does the world ignore our pain?

Countless young sisters with blown up stomachs
Left alone to birth a nation
Long lost days of innocence
Have we forgotten freedom's proclamation?
Two hundred years later
And we're still fighting to be free
Peace is the beast that eludes us
If you could only see

I *Wonder*

Raised rough in the streets, all the while I dreamt of those brighter tomorrows
Damned near a victim to that senseless black on black crime
In order to make it out, I had to rise above the spiritual degradation and sorrow
No father around to teach me the simple things, like how to whistle
Nor was there a guiding hand teaching me how to shave
So many nights I would have to journey to that spiritual place
On the vision quest searching for the Shaman like an Indian Brave
But it was during my many moments of isolation that I would often wonder
Why was the abuse and neglect like nitro pumping through my veins?
The pain in my brain was loud, and at times I can still hear the thunder

My mother worked tirelessly, trying to give us all that she could
She sacrificed self to no end, never questioning if whether she should
Please forgive me now mother, because at times as a child
I'm sure that I couldn't have understood
That you had to hustle to bring home the bacon
She felt the omnipresent weight of pressure because she had three mouths to feed
And like her strongest warrior or her greatest protector
When she'd breakdown to cry I'd die a thousand deaths
My spirit would become rage filled, or worse, my heart would bleed

At times even now though I'm a man both strong and courageous
I fight against those demons, because spiritual poverty can be so voracious
At times I find myself sitting in circumspect, I often ask
Why my biological father never bothered to step up
Why he decided not to bother, I often wonder
The pain in my brain was loud, and at times I can still hear the thunder

Majuscule Angst

I have been removed from the gutter for about ten years now
And I no longer see the faces of my long buried peers
Tenuous is our savage living
I see the trepidation in the faces of our grandparents, it's easy to sense their fear
So many reports of hapless violent deaths already this year
Expired lost precious lives, of those who thought to risk life to win it all
The names of those ghetto born immortalized street soldiers
Names tattooed on their comrade's arms or plastered in graffiti on the walls
Lost jewels gone to never return, they are now all legends of the fall

It's because of my people's contrite living, that I possess this magnified frustration
My soul is cloaked under a blanket of both pain and anger
Because we are creeping ever so closely to extinction
Our existence has been driven to the brink of genocidal expiration
It is in this the 21st century that my people hold that fratricidal distinction
We are in a battle with our own mortality, and in due form we stand face to face
Perilously we are losing the war with our truest enemy, ourselves
And this is why my heart is filled with such majuscule angst

Mannequins on Parade

As a teen I would see visages of ghost like crack fiends
Aimless they would march, but they were more like mannequins on parade
Hapless hopeless victims, a legion of the un-dead
People with great potential who fell under the oppression of Cocaine's vicious tirade
Long lost souls, these people decided that just once
They'd curiously taste what they thought would be sweetness
But instead what they found was hell encapsulated in Cocaine's powdery death
They have become a collective of invisible transients
Who awaits the moment of their final cocaine induced caustic breath
Now that I am more conscious of this social pariah
I am more able to see the full view of Cocaine's destructive display
Minds finding moments marred, memories are forgotten
Brains become lumps of un-necessary matter like formless useless clay
Cocaine fiends delving devilishly downward
Committing acts of desperation for this hell born debasing crop
Tears fill the eyes of all in the world
As we question if whether or not the madness will ever stop

I believe that it is in our brotherhood of man, whereby we will truly save our people
Which makes more viable the mantra, *"He ain't heavy, he's my brother"*
We must again find that we believe in the words of such a powerful creed
We must pray for deliverance in this land of plenty
We must stand students to history, centuries worth of warnings that we must heed
If we look close enough, we'll stand witness to a nation of babies who cry out
This slaughter of the innocence must stop now
We must acknowledge their voluminous pleads
Futures forsaken forever, held captive by Cocaine's scrupulous deeds
Crack cocaine is only second to the atom bomb
In being the most destructive product man has ever made
We must fight for those who can't, those misguided mannequins on parade

Perceptions

I see you little boy shackled to the arm of the chair
Unbeknownst to you, your life has become reduced to one of dread and despair
Un-cleansed for days at a time, your body is attacked by miniscule minions
You are a victim to time as you are battered by each minute's opinion
Only allowed food twice during the day
Your body becomes emaciated as you slowly slip away
You exist in a mind state of futility, as you possess no visions of tomorrow
The moments of your life are passing by scattered
You sit with bated breath, inhaling and exhaling
Both of these actions seem so measured and borrowed
You are not allowed to use your imagination or to have joyful displays
So you seek solace in your secret mental garden
And its there that you find focus enough to pray

I see you little boy shackled to the arm of the chair
They medicate you claiming that you don't have the span for prolonged attention
When you find a reason to act out, you are locked away
Out of sight, out of mind, your name is rarely if ever mentioned
They tell you, *"here take these pills, they'll calm and relax you"*
Lest they forget that you were locked away in a world
Where your sanity is refused, ugly is the word that describes how they abuse you
Still you pray asking God to, *"forgive them, for they know not what they do"*
Listen to me through telepathy little boy shackled to the arm of the chair
Find freedom's pathway in your mind, and escape their dungeon like prison
Their incorrect prognosis begets money, and you are a victim to this deception
False prescriptions is their true crime and mangled are their devilish perceptions

Poetic Explosion

I've studied the Art of War scripts transcribed onto ancient strips of bamboo
Authored by the wizardry of the Chinese General and philosopher Sun Tzu
I've walked the halls of learning, scaling the walls of the ghetto logic of Iceberg Slim
I am the corrupted seed of an adulterous father and a disillusioned mother
Who during a moment of sin filled passion, made me on a lustful whim
I've searched the paradoxes planted in my conscience
For a momentary glimpse of my destiny chamber
As I find it, I see that it's labeled in bright red— *"Warning-Militant Zone-Danger!"*

I step into this chamber filled with excitement and
I'm overcome with a quest beginning like thrill
Though up ahead I see the foreboding form taking shape
Of what seems to be an impregnable mountainous hill
But I know that to deal with the many hurdles that I'll face
I'll have to use every ounce of my Heaven sent will
So I'll climb along undauntedly
Battling all demons that may arise with my impervious empyreal zeal

My destiny was to do battle with Legion, even on the battlefields in the belly of hell
I will traverse the terrain of the jungle, stumble I may, but I'm not afraid to fail
I have been sent by God, forever will I rise only expecting to excel
I have no choice but to build a strong powerful legacy
All the while my deeds will bolster the days of mine own life's tale
While utilizing prose and verse to create a finite literary potion
Searching the Guff for wisdom, powered by an intellectual propulsion
Increasing my strength and skill all the while
Preparing for the battle readily, while on the quest for a poetic explosion

Quintessential Belief

The prophet says that *"The meek shall inherit the earth"*
This scripture filled indoctrination begins at the moment of our birth
We were once a people labeled as expendable chattel
As our fates were decided by our genetic make-up
This is what determined the amount of your worth
We once played the guinea pig for a scientific experiment
As they searched for the truths about syphilis
We played the role of the sacrificial lamb
We were snatched against our desires
And delivered unto this once savage land
We were a people who were openly ridiculed, ostracized and totally divided
Once set on the path toward destruction
Willie Lynch's letter almost guaranteed that we would never again stand united
We have lost so many lives to lynchings and senseless killings
And as a result of which, our greatest rage had been ignited

It is now during this current day where living as a black man can leave you in peril
This is evidenced in that you can find
So many of our men stashed away in the penitentiaries
Which stand as 21st century zoos
Full of African, Mexican and Native Americans
Who could barely survive by society's rules?
Yet when we listen close to their perpetual cries for freedom
"Live trapped or die free…you choose!"
So for now we sit watching the sky, searching for signs of relief
"The meek shall inherit the earth", this is our one remaining quintessential belief

Sambo Syndrome

As a people we've dealt with having men in our tribe
Who are deplete of strength, for there was no honor laden in their hearts
Too scared to accept their roles as Kings
They had no understanding of how to play their parts
Instead of demanding change, they happily greeted the oppressor
They were content with their passivity
Too fearful to assume the role of the aggressor

These men put on their lawn jockey uniforms
And eagerly painted their faces up like clowns
They were not cherished because of their intellect
They weren't worth more than their Massa's hounds
They gleefully sold out their people
And were pleased to be considered unequal
They almost ruined the images of us as regal
With a lack of character which was near lethal
They forgot that once upon a time we ascended the throne
So pandemic was this sickness, that we call the sambo syndrome

See What I See

DuBois, Nat Turner, Denmark Vescey and Garvey
Tienamen Square, Hiroshima, Rwanda and Kosovo
Mahatma, King and the Kennedys
All relevant because they were all driven by one common drive
Theirs was a mission, to insure that freedom would forever remain alive
Can you see what I do see?
There's a heavy burden to pay, for even freedom isn't free

Oppression still lingers over this world's head
It's a ravenous beast, a truly forebodding creature
You become the meal at the feast
Where to live free is the feature
Malcom, Mandela, Guevara and Lorca
Can you see what I do see?
That freedom bears the cross, for even freedom isn't free

Southern Calm

Let's talk for a minute about the southern calm
Its destructive power was like that of the neutron bomb
It spread throughout the south as if it were napalm
It was as strong a belief to them, as was the book of Psalms
It was said that slavery happened as a result of
The once African savages needing Christianity
How arrogant to connect God to that wicked insanity
It makes one ask, in order to teach Christianity
Does it take whips and chains?
Slavery happened to free the white colonialist
From those very harsh labor pains
Evidence of the southern calm was often found
Hanging in the poplar trees
It sent cowards who were blanketed under white hooded sheets
On many unlawful killing sprees
It was as detrimental for the world
As was the Holocaust atrocity
Some say slavery never happened
Others say, *"Get over it"* because it's a part of our history
The southern calm was a stain on our country
And it has left our nation nearly lost and empty

Tales from an Urban Realist

Modern day Poets, some are hip-hop soloist
Literate works akin to Cezanne or Michaelangelo
The unequaled genius that flows from the mind
Of these inner city impressionist
Expressions of an environment beset on the path of eternal woes
With the gift to tell the urban tales
Allegories set in concrete, delivered from within the eye of the teller
Blessed with the gift of prophetic poignancy
Akin to that of the re-known Ms. Helen Keller
Vast is the intellectual power that's stored in their mental cellars

Stories so descript, of a community fighting within itself
Seeming to move so expeditiously toward its ultimate destruction
A plan formulated at the moment of emancipation
America's most hypocritical ultimate corruption
Although some white men never thought then
That it would ever affect them
Our realities are forever intertwined
By the stroke of Lincoln's pen

No more Negro spirituals or singing those inspiring Heavenly gospels
The voice of the new age literati is enforced with a mentality that's hostile
We need to continue to search the skies for that God sent light
Especially during this age of urban realism
We are a people in so much need
Thirsting for a 21st century sense of that ever elusive heroism

The Ledge

Lessons made innate because of their father's fate
Will we ever be saved or will the Dove of peace arrive too late?
Divine intervention seems to be our only hope
Save the children Lord, from the violence, self hate and dope
My duty is just to teach one to lead a nation
To show him the greatness, with each new day begun
Because when I face my creator
The only question that I may have to answer is
"To help change the world, what have you done?"

My pledge is to stand on the wall
And to fight from the ledge
To save our children
I will be their protective hedge
He did it for me; He died so that I could live free
And what is it that I must give back?
My everything, that thing which makes me…me
Allow my sweat and tears to gather, to be forged into a sword of steel
Let my deeds bring forth my wings
To deliver me to the top of the hill
Equip me for the battle Lord
Strengthen my unconquerable Heaven sent will
Empower my soul for the pilgrimage
And take me home if I should fall on the battlefield
I will go it alone if I must, I will be your single soldier army
Just continue to guide me like You have done my whole life long
Make ready my shield and sword, so nothing can ever harm me

Venom

Subtle but deadly like the bite of a Rattlesnake
It paralyzes a man's character
And ultimately, it causes his heart to break
It flows from one person's mouth
Into the ear of anyone that would listen
It seeks to destroy the soul of its victim
This is Venom's nefariously wicked mission

Venom acts fast, and it cuts into the flesh of a person's integrity
A level of integrity that took years to build
Venom filled words flow from snakes personified
And they are members of the Viper's Guild
Venom are words so powerful and potent
That they lead to a silent kill
Words created by people bitter for the sake of being bitter
People who could care less how
Their poison makes another feel

Venom has helped to propel the worst of
Man's inhumanity to man
Words that destroy the power of
Our most elaborately drafted plans
Venom for some unfortunately are the
Only words that they will ever understand
How do we stop Venom's destruction?
Where does Venom's hate come from?
It's the most powerful form of chemical warfare
Words that we call Venom

Prologue ... The Reflection

It was when I was nearing my late twenties that I started having revelations. It was during these days of reflection that I started seeing the lighter side of life. It was also during those days that I started seeking a closer walk with God, which of course made me take a closer look at myself and the man that I was becoming. I realized that before I could work on the creation of a better me, with God's help and guidance of course, I would need to reflect on my life's journey and what it meant to me. I had to take stock in my bad decisions and I had to find a place of peace within them. I had to ask for forgiveness for the decisions that I made that would ultimately impact the lives of others, and I had to apologize in advance for the decisions that wouldn't be so great, that I would make in my future, for everyday we sit in the classroom called life, and we are going to make mistakes. It is our duty to learn from those mistakes and to become better human beings because of them, or else, they would be for naught, with no lessons taught.

As I began my journey of reflection, I found that I was also having a moment of reprieve. I found that as I thought about how hard my life's journey had begun, I realized that I hadn't truly experienced any real and true peace and I knew that this dynamic would have to change, though I knew that ultimately I would first have to make peace about my past, and then I would have to ask God for a true and peaceful re-commencement to my life. No, I didn't want to have not have lived those moments, but I wanted to capitalize on them and learn from them, so that the next thirty-five years, God willing, would be as peaceful as possible. I also started having moments of realization during this reflection. I realized that I would have to begin forgiving those who had wronged me, during my lifetime up to that juncture. I would have to let go of that baggage if I was to truly move on with my life, moving on toward those days of higher peace and tranquility. I would have to let go of the pain of being told by that gentleman who worked at the same contracting company that I worked at during my summers while I was in high school. I had to forgive him for telling me that I couldn't be an attorney because I wasn't smart enough. I remember how he told me, *"You could always be a janitor just like me. This is one of the last true honorable jobs left in this country, but you are definitely not smart enough to be a lawyer, or anything else"* What's amazing is how life just has a way of bringing things full circle. I say that because, I saw this same gentleman years later one day when I happened to be at the pet store buying some food for my exotic fish and there he walked in. I recognized him immediately because he still looked the same, except for the fact that he has lost some hair, and because of the janitor's uniform showcasing his last name was what brought his identity home for me. I walked up to him and confirmed that it was him first, asking him, if he was Mr. so and so, and he confirmed that yes he was, and then I asked him if he worked at that old contracting company and he again said yes, and then I asked him if he remembered me, and he of course said no. Not to belabor the moment, I looked him square in the eye and told him that I remembered him and that I wanted to thank him for what he had said to me those many years prior.

I told him eagerly, that I was so thankful for him telling me that I wasn't smart enough to become an attorney and I thanked him for telling me that I wouldn't amount to much, though in essence, he didn't even know me. He knew nothing about me, but that didn't matter. What mattered was that he had the sad gall to tell a teenager that he wouldn't amount to much of nothing. So, I thanked him for planting that fire deep inside of my soul's well, and that when I needed to draw on that fuel for strength, I would often think about his words and then I would press onward, toward the successful accomplishing of whatever goal was at hand. After having said this to him, I shook his hand and walked away, only to look back and to see him standing there with a dire look of woe about him.

I didn't hold anything against this man, and I was truly thankful for the role that he had played in my life, but it was time to let it go. It was time to move forward and to progress toward my life's truest purpose. I remember thinking that I had a lot to ask for forgiveness for and I knew that God was listening, because the more that I asked for forgiveness, the lighter the weight of my heart became. I was no longer held captive to thoughts grounded in hostility. No more did I feel a need to have my spirit fueled by anger and I was thankful for that release. I was starting to receive the gift of deliverance from God and I rejoiced.

From that moment forward, I started to advise everyone, to just let the things that were burdening them, go. I told them that, their reward would be a greater sense of peace and that the only thing that would hold them back from this spirit of peace was themselves and I must admit that, I truly am appreciative of the spirit of peace that I am experiencing because, without it, I would not have had a vision clear enough and free from blurriness to move forward in life.

The Reflection

Alive

Imagine that you are walking down life's pathway
As you step, you notice that its foundation is not made of stone or clay
While on this journey, you may feel as if you're all alone
As you step, you begin staring at the walls of the pathway
And you see that the movie called, *"This is your life"* is being shown
With each step you realize that you see no signs of life
And this creates the sensation of total desolation
You suddenly call out, *"is there anyone out there!?"*
This of course is a futile act caused by intense desperation
As you continue forward, you start feeling
As if you are being restrained by a cold unyielding grip
And you suddenly feel as if you can't breathe
While on the inside your spirit cries out, longing to be free

Then all at once your survival instinct tells you to calm yourself
And then freedom becomes your purpose driven mission
You focus for a minute as your eyes search the darkness for the light
Innately guided by your God sent intrinsic intuition
You steady yourself as you regain your stride
You find that you are approaching a cliff
With what seems to be a mile of water
Dividing you from the other side
You begin to circumspect, thinking about your life
Wondering what might have led you to this day
As you postulate about what it will take to get across
You question yourself, *"should I jump, or should I stay?"*
Then faintly you hear the whispers
Telling you that this water represents new life
And you again wonder if whether or not you should dive
Then courage finds you and you poise yourself, then you leap
"Splash!" and in an instant you begin to feel alive

An Infinite Peace

An infinite peace is what I'm searching for
To enter the peace dimension is what I'm questing for
It is the energizing source of life, this golden bowl that we call peace
I have long desired to stop traveling through Hell's domain
I have fallen to my knees humbly asking God for deliverance from the pain
I have pictured peace as a tranquil crystal clear lake
Or yet a quiet room filled with silence, which the slightest noise couldn't break
I have always thought that in order to experience peace
That I would have to fall into the kind of trance
That a slow lulling daze, that only a summer day tends to make
Peace is hypnotically heavy when it's in its most ethereal state
Think of the mesmerizing affect of the music
That only Robin Thicke can create

Tonight I fall asleep searching, for I know that it's somewhere out there
If I find it, how do I harness it, or should I even dare?
Peace is like the stallion is wild, it with its hyper kinetic air
It's the constant never ending grind demanding that I slow down
The daily drive to better my standard of living
Is why my feet pounds the ground
I may forever chase this dream, my destiny commands me to never cease
I may never stop searching for that inner utopia
Nirvana is the oasis that I sojourn for
Its hidden treasure is an infinite peace

Baobab Shade

The uttermost arid places in Africa house the ancient Baobab tree
It's where the Lions find a respite, and the Gorillas dance free
It's where the Shaman would seek God's power
And it's where the Hyena would come to play
It's where the Zulu and the Bantu seem to have it made
For they can literally taste the richness in the air
While sitting in the Baobab's shade

Desire

To scale the mountain with all that I've got
The prize is simple, the summit of the mountaintop
To run in that marathon until I can take no more as my body nearly drops
Until my lungs are at capacity and I can almost feel my heart stop
It pushes me like a Drill Sergeant
Expecting my all as it demands my very best
It is the very thing that forces me to enter the zone to introspect
Looking deep within my soul with a surgeon's like circumspection
It is what guides me to the crossroads
Where I find that all roads meet at an intersection

It is the inextinguishable impervious fire
God placed into us all, this thing we call desire
It commands that I turn to face and embrace my fear
And to go that extra mile to make that sale
It ignites the torch within, driving me to succeed
And yet it reminds me to never be afraid to fail
It is the best part of me that I wish to pass on to my progeny
It forces me to study every fiber and sinewy part of my ontology
It is the only part of my being that affects how I chase my destiny
It is the truest nexus that bridges all of the rest of me
It is the inexplicable lucid presence that I see
Standing before me when the journey makes me tire
It is at that moment that I know that God is near
And I pray that He sees my desire

Echoes

At times when all is silent, I can hear the whispers calling me
Poets from the past challenging me to step out on faith
Their insolence demands, *"Be what you know you ought to be!"*
It's as if they know that poetry is the one thing that sets me free
It is the pristine view of the canopy; it is the calm waters of the sea

The whispers I speak of come from my many Poet models
Langston Hughes, Gil Scott-Herron, Garcia Lorca and Richard Wright
Their spirits visit me in the darkness, and they guide me toward the light
They have taught me that, *"When it comes to rules in poetry, there are none"*
They say, *"Whether it's iambic pentameter, or haiku, just remember to have fun"*
I have learned that the only thing that matters in regards to this art form
Is that you must have a passion for the written prose
So, I am thankful for the guidance filled ancestral whispers
And for the mystical power of those ethereal Poetic echoes

If I Could

If I could repaint the world, I'd do it with the fluid hand of Goya
Or the adverse perfectly abstract eye of the legendary Picasso
Give me skills equal to the incomparable Cezanne
Or grant me the mystic artistic understanding of Michaelangelo
Allow me to sit at the feet of the master Monet
Or let me possess the spirit of Vincent Van Gogh
Is it too much to roll them all into one celestial flame
And to place it deep within the depths of my poetic soul

If I could re-teach the world, I'll need the patience of Mandela
And the fiery will of Malcolm Little
Allow me to reach and inspire the world as did JFK and Dr. King
Give me strength coupled with the spirit to stand for the artistic cause
Akin to the unrelenting endurance of Mahatma Ghandi
Who like Brother Martin had a dream
And lastly, anoint me with a rebellious grace to speak through my actions
As did Peter Benenson, Muhammad Ali and Cesar Chavez
This world could be a better place if we all strive to make it that way
This is what the spirits of these collective legends says
I will do my part to help change the world
Though the perils of that journey is well understood
I just want to affect change through peace, if I could

Imagination

As I gaze out across the horizon, I'm imagining that I'm
Riding through the streets of Milan on my antique Vespa
Clad in my black Armani suit, seeking to walk in the steps of
The Italian renaissance artists stride for stride
In my mind's eye, I'm in the center of Rome's Coliseum
And it's on the back of the bull that I ride
I'm on the journey to catch the most grandest of oysters
Whose gift is the freedom pearl
I have made the Haj to the most amazing places on this world
I have stood under the Arc de Triumph
And I have kneeled in the center of the Pyramids at Giza
I have leaped from the cliff of inhibition
And I have traversed the frozen tundra of the Antartic
Where to find the lost tribe of the Ice Men was my mission
In my mind I have traveled to that most arid place called the Skeleton Coast
I have gripped the hands of Shackleford, DuSable and Livingston
I have shaken off the shingles of stagnation
Simply by using the gift of my imagination

Inner Suffrage

Was I cursed from the moment of my creation?
Meant to drown in my primordial genetic cesspool
If I collided with the world around me
Would I be locked in a destructive eternal duel?
Was I sent here to never rest, wandering through life on the warpath?
If I conquered the world or it conquered me, what would be the aftermath?
Am I caught up in this maze because of the sins of my adulterous father?
Am I meant to forever search for a definitive masculine model?
Questioning why he who planted the seed never bothered
As I meet people along this walk, I often question if whether they are friend or foe
Curious of what lies on the other side of their facial mask, for only God knows

In these days of dazes, in what inkling of man can I learn to trust?
I have surmised those who are the two legged cannibal animals
Whose every desire is to conquer and crush
That's their life affirming action, and the source of their hyperbolic rush
For they unfortunately conquer not for sport, but to exist they must
Man has become royally complacent, for in our dominion
We are bound and snared by a cataclysmically destructive chain
But once we have perished all of our natural resources
What will be the need for our dominion, what world will remain?
As I awake in the morning and fall to my knees to pray
I beseech God to give me power, for to help change the world is my pledge
Man knows all too well the inhumanity we serve unto one another
And this is the source of our own eternal inner suffrage

Kindred

It has been said that we each have a twin, maybe in some other universal plane
Some may allow this statement to drive their curiosity
Others may react with a hint of disdain
But for those who believe, this may begin a search that last eternal
Not knowing if this twin is a carbon copy, or if this twin is fraternal
But me, I believe that I will one day meet mine
Will this kindred spirit be strong like the wolf
Or will she be cryptically and strongly feline?
It will feel mystical and third dimensional
The way that our spirits will be intertwined
My sixth sense tells me that she'll be here soon
A message delivered to me so extrasensory sublime

I believe that her spirit will be poetic, driven by a total literary understanding
Her actions will call out for equality in this world
Justice and peace will be the truths that she'll be demanding
She will be a modern day version of the French heroine Joan
Us two against the world, our minds will mesh into one
While we exist in this cryptically quixotic zone
Will we together change the world?
Only God knows
But we'll pray that our lives will create a legacy
Created by our twin kindred souls

Love

It is as fleeting as a flock of sparrows
It can make you feel as if you are flying in wide open spaces
It can take you to the loneliest chambers of your heart
To the worst of the cold dark places
It is the one thing, only second to God
That can bring the strongest man to his knees
It can make the hard at heart cry out loud, beg and plead
Love is the one intangible, on which our hearts feed
And in order to live, it is the one thing that we all need

Love will make you walk the Earth, reaching for its farthest regions
Believe them when they say, that love has no true rhyme or reason
Love is the one thing that can never be possessed
Love is in fact, the hardest of life's many tests
To win the love of the woman that a man desires
Love will convince him that he is impregnable
Making him believe that he can walk across fire
Love can make a woman see the real soul of a man
And beyond all of his faults
Love compels her to share her world with him
Her inner most dreams and thoughts
Love for me has been my greatest inspiration
It is my truest source of found moments of emancipation
For Love has sought to set me free
She has given me the cup of life
And that's what Love has done for me

Marooned

A moment of serene reflection seems to be gripping my mind
As this calm Caribbean wind affects my mood, it compels me to unwind
As I stare out across the ocean, it appears as though the spirit of peace
Languishes just above the sea's non-existent torrent
I'm sitting on the edge of beautiful, and this moment is time well spent
I'm a castaway, and slowly blown about across this vast liquefied plane
As I sit back and watch this harmony filled journey unfold
I am awed by the power of God, and His ability to create such a tranquil terrain
As I simplistically coast along, in what feels like slow motion
Memories of wonderful start to float through the chambers in my brain
Visions of romantic acts seem to fuel passion's uncontrollable flame
There is nothing more I need, than a night kissed by a tropical breeze
I am overcome with the power of this vision, and I meekly fall to my knees
This place has allowed me entry into my celestial listening room
And I now have been rescued, from being emotionally marooned

No Quest, No Glory

I'm up at the break of dawn, once again to happily greet the Sun
I hit my knees to pray for forgiveness
For any trespassing that I may have done
Then my soul becomes energized
And this energy increases the strength of my spirit
Emboldened to stand my post at Heaven's gate
Ready to battle all demons that try to come near it
Legion tries to disguise himself, but he can't hide his hooves and horns
His body armor is near impenetrable
Created to protect him from Heaven's girding thorns

While standing on post, I suddenly hear the Angels
Sounding their warning trumpets, declaring a celestial war
Gabriel comes running yielding his battering ram
With the style and strength akin to the Norse mythological hero Thor
The battle commences as we collide
With a vicious force from Hell's sentinel legion
We fight to ensure that the people of God will forever exist
For we have now entered into Hell's hunting season

Is Heaven due to have an apocalypse of its own?
Will the Devil defeat the Golden Forces, capturing the Heavenly throne?
At the beginning of this battle, my vision was both cloudy and blurry
It was that my sight was marred by my intense fierce fury
Though mortal man may not recall the accounts of this near cataclysmic story
The Angels will remember the evoking power of the battle cry from the Arch Angel
Michael's summoning exclamation resounding out loud, *"No Quest, No Glory!"*

Nowhere to Hide

When it comes down to it, there is nowhere to hide
Sometimes the pain can be so surreal, don't keep it on the inside
Depression is such an oppressive monster
But you must stand and fight to remain free
Trust in who made you and believe in the light that you see
I know that people counted you out
And that they left you standing alone by yourself in the wild
The world around us can be so negatively infectious
Infected days of lost innocence, left behind with your days as a child
One million miles away, sometimes peace may seem
But hold on to tomorrow, and dream the perfect dream
No matter what those around you might say
No matter how much they persecute you for righteousness sake
It doesn't matter how they try to destroy your spirit or try to degrade
They can't take away from God's greatness that flows in you
For at your moment of creation, no mistakes were made
You were sent here to be all that you were designed to be
The Grand Architect drafted the blueprint, which makes you totally unique
And He gave His only begotten Son, in order that you may live free
Just stand immovable, and focus your heart to persevere and strive
And let the golden rays of Heaven remind you, that you are so very much alive

October Moon

You speak to me with your rhythmic moods
I hear the drums beat when the leaves fall to the ground
The average person can't hear them but I do
Each and every resonating sound
As the nights draw near, in this my favorite month
My heart grows wild as it starts to beat and pound
And when the moon finally rises my soul becomes
Immersed by the spirit of the wolf, I start to bay and howl
The moon transforms me into a different me
The me, that's totally free and wild
Oh, how the gravitational pull tugs strongly at my heart
I'm like a curious wolf cub, or more like a carefree child
I am commanded to act by this celestial body
I am driven to create by her beams, done so without reason or rhyme
It's like floating empirically, through the caverns of my mind
And with each approaching new day begun
My night's journey is destined to end soon
My spirit ascends toward the sky
Guided by my mystic ties with each October Moon

Pencil Me In

I write to release
I write to find peace
I write to add to the voice
I write because I have no choice
I write to say what I feel
I write about things true and real
I know that I have been blessed with this ability to write the way that I do
I write because I'm in search of the ever elusive unchanging truth
I write not just for me, but I write for you too
I'm not one of those writers who write only when I feel blue
Often when I sit down with a piece of paper, and a pencil or a pen
I journey to a different world and I search for a spiritual place to begin
Then I'm compelled to start by that so very familiar voice
And it's then that my gift begins to transcend
It's my spirit speaking to me, and it says, *"I'm here, so pencil me in"*

Quest Eternal

I catch myself in circumspect pondering
While on a wraithlike cosmic ride
Lost but happily wandering
As I contemplate about my life and times
Searching for a glimpse of my future
Eagerly anticipating about what I might find
Will my horizons be laced with doubt delivering gray clouds?
Or will I see old familiar faces, in a warm friendly crowd?
I've found comfort in my belief in both righteousness and love
This way when St. Peter welcomes me home
The Angels will release the peace filled doves
I catch myself in circumspect postulating
Asking the Lord to deliver me, while I kneel in prayer
I have visions of me soaring across the sanctuary granting skies
While I'm riding on the back of a winged beautiful black mare
But until I have met the event of my demise
I claim dominion over this world, for this is my birthright due
I'll quest eternal until I'm gone
Seeking to capture that never ending truth

Solace in Blue

I find my solace in blue
A tint that is more than a color for me
For she possesses the mystical gift to heal and soothe
I find my solace in blue
Her with her powers to soothe, often controls my mood
In any shade or tone, she's my most beloved hue
And that's why I feel as though I have found Heaven
When I have found my solace in blue

Song of the Medieval Sage

He was born deep in the depths of the Earth's core
Driven from the moment of his genesis
He lived his life knowing what his future was to have in store
He was forced to see the face of death long before death arrived
In the form of the pestilence driven black plague
Listen closely to his heart's rhythm, for this is the song of the medieval sage
You see the world truthfully, as your wisdom flows and grows
You record the dynamics of history, through the creation of lyrical prose

As a result of having a mind's eye that can sense what's imminent
You are often sadden by the fate of the world's future days
Listen to the lyrics of this poetry, for this is the song of the medieval sage
That lived his life in a panoramic daze
He would travel this world, traversing its maze
Died after having lived a life well spent
All that he requested was that his body be set ablaze
He passed to the great beyond after having created an incredible legacy
Though now, no more is the song of the medieval sage

Soulful Eyes

My grandmother has the softest brown eyes
And at her age, she has seen so many skies
If there ever were a, 'Most Beautiful Eyes' contest
Barbara would definitely win first prize
Those eyes have the power to scorn you with just one look
Those eyes have the power to make you feel penalized
Ultimately leaving you feeling equally derided and shook
My grandmother has the most awesomely powerful piercing eyes
You can see God's goodness in them, which would make you realize
That Granny was sent here from Heaven, by the hand of the Most High
My grandmother has the most awesomely beautiful softest brown eyes
I think of the magic that they've seen, and then I start to surmise
That Granny has both a wealth of knowledge
And experience stored, within those soulful eyes

Sphinxman

We first met on that cool October night
And we made a vow to be brothers fraternally
Though we didn't know it then, we soon found out
That this promise would be written in blood, sweat and tears
And this fluid would connect us eternally
We had no idea of what the journey would be like
We just followed the leader, compelled to do so
Because it simply felt right
We started out as Alpha Men of Tomorrow
And we quickly found out that it would be
Each other's strength upon which we would lean and borrow
As the days would pass while on that quest
We truly would come to count on one another
More than we ever thought we would
Ours was a bond bound by honor
And to operate with an air of regal distinction was expected and understood
The test would come, hard and heavy everyday
But that didn't matter, for we truly had each other's backs
The man in front with the slightest stature led the pack
The 'Bloodline' tried to break us down with all of their might
As was done to them by the men from the 'Lords of the Light'
Thoroughly was the fraternal history engrained into us all
With the motivating belief that one day we'd shout that "06!" call
We were guided by our most honorable conductor
Our Dean Bullet to that black and old gold land
To beg for entrance through the gates, was our united plan
Then there in the cold dark pit of that, our longest hour
We crossed the mighty Nile River and
Entered the oasis as Sphinxmen while on our knees and hands
The quest was finally over and we found a moment to sojourn as we started to chant
    "Go down, brothers, way down to Egyptland"
"And tell old, Pharaoh, to let you crossed those sands"
And to this day I carry with me, the pride of being an Alpha Man

Still I *Search*

Gazing out just above the horizon
Though I'm not sure of what I'm looking for
At this moment I have a small semblance of peace
But like a starved beast, I hunger for more
I am caught between the canopy and the carpet of
A blue sky and sawdust colored sand
For I know that it's on the edge between
Chaotic humanity and peaceful serenity that I stand
I close my eyes and floating cherubs
Comes to my mind and I begin to feel at ease
It's as calming an affect as is a beautiful fall day
When the wind softly blows about the fallen leaves
Again, I'm not sure of why I search, but I feel a need to be free
Suddenly I open my eyes and then it stops
The skies even stop rolling past the mountain tops
There is nothing calm about the plane, that exist between Heaven and Earth
And for now I know that it may forever elude me, but still, I search

Still Steppin'

Here I stand, a once broken man
I'm climbing the mountain
Doing the best that I can
No lows, no hurdles can slow me down
I'm on the pursuit of that golden crown
I may tire, and I may stumble and fall
So many lessons in my life
Though ultimately, I learned to stand tall
I'm on the quest, and I'm both humble and hungry
I've seen the source of my power, and in my dreams it haunts me
I have the vision and I see me standing on top of the mountain high
I'll leap from the edge of the cliff, and with these wings I will fly
I'll take a second and I'll smile at the sun, as I'm soaring by
I've been delivered, I've settled all debts and
I am he who has been saved, so I'll keep on steppin'

Take Me There

Take me there, to that place of
Respite found on this lazy hazy Sunday
Relaxation realized deep within the
Walls of my listening room
So melodic is the tune, propelled by
The musical genius of Maxwell and a glass of mimosa
All stress gone and expired by a healthy dose of
No pandering, pondering or solicitation of
Any supposedly important notion
Delivered from all weighty burdens by
The strength of this peace filled potion

I listen intently as I am coolly calmed by the
Calming affect of the music created by Norman Brown
A truly gifted and awe compelling musician
Those are big words that express an easy feeling made so real
Because of my feelings that I'm being confounded by the most skilled magician
I have been rescued from the world's hectic rat race
The warmth of these summer breezes seems to be slowing my mind's pace
I am a victim no more to the daily wheeling and dealing
Take me there to that land called harmony
And rejuvenate me by the beauty of its calm tranquil healing

The Moon Can Do

As I sit here gazing out over the moon lit ocean
While sitting in this relaxing chair
I watch her slowly move about
As the wind gently kisses her hair
I suddenly feel the grip of a tropical breeze as it strolls on in
I feel the Moon's healing powers, for I have wounds to mend
As she talks, I stare at her lips looking seductive and I am moved
Those lips are captured and cloaked in a soft ice blue hue
As the sheer shade wilts in and out
This moment of calm has removed all stress and doubt
We become totally zombie like because of the reverie from the
Eclectically soulful sounds of Eric Roberson as he sets the mood
I have fallen victim to the things that the Moon can do
She has delivered me, and it's my soul that she soothes

This Poet's Soul

Often tormented and tested, though somehow it's mysteriously nurtured
Expressions flow from ink, and my inner world is perjured
Moments of found strength gained from my life's lessons
My soul is blanketed under a collage of, moving poetic expressions
I exclaim my desire for peace, when I bridge verbs and nouns
To become a purveyor of peace and its pathway is what I have found
Helping to heal the world through the creation of prose
Yet it remains the eternal enigma, the strength of this poet's soul

Venice Streets

In my mind I have traveled to Venice, where the streets are liquefied
To experience Venice's beauty and revelry, one should not be denied
Instead of thinking that you'd have to deal with
All of the hustle, bustle and pollution from street cars
The Venice mode of transportation seems to simply glide
In my mind I have traveled to Venice where
Instead of street lights, the gondolas meet
I so look forward to the day, that I can travel those Venice streets

Write On Blue

When I dream, I see shades of blue
The mood is cool like the legendary poet Sekou
My dreams are affected by blue's varying hues
And I am comforted by whichever hue I choose
Blue seems to possess a melodic smooth groove
It with its mystical rhythm has
The power to both move and soothe
Blue can be hot, warm or cold
Just think of the warmth found in indigo
Blue is the source of my heart's song flow
Blue empowers my poetically passionate pit
And that pit happens to be my lyric filled soul

Prologue ... The Redemption

I, like many, have so many things to be thankful for. I am thankful for being alive. I am thankful for having the knowledge of who made me. I am thankful for the indomitable spirit that was infused into my being at the moment of my genesis. I am thankful for being blessed with a vision for what my life was and is to mean. I am thankful for the incredible will and strength that He has given me. I am thankful for having survived so many snares and toils. I am thankful that He centered me in such a strong familial lineage. I am thankful for all of the opportunities that He has blessed me with. I am thankful for the two sons that He has given me and I know that He expects me to develop them into men of character, as I provide stewardship over my sons. I am also thankful for the continued forgiveness that He grants me everyday.

I believe that in my 35 years of living, I have made so many mistakes, some knowingly, though with no desire to hurt or trespass against anyone. I have also made some mistakes because of my desire to succeed, which has actually allowed me to learn some harsh lessons. I am thankful for those lessons, and I know that it is through these lessons, that wisdom is given. I feel that being thankful is not enough and that a person must couple that thankful spirit, with the desire to find atonement and redemption for the not so righteous deeds that are committed along life's journey. That's my quest, redemption.

Redemption is defined as, *"being saved from sin"* according to Webster's Dictionary. I know that my journey intensifies and that the stronger test begins now. I have known my whole life, that I was sent here for a reason and I have learned that in order to capture and to embrace that reason, I had better fall to my knees seeking and beseeching God's grace, asking Him to grant me redemption. In order to become the he that God planned for me to be, I better seek redemption, though I am forever mindful that I am not perfect. I am as flaw filled as the next man, but like all men, I am chasing the example of the one true perfect being and I chase that example with fervor.

I believe that men undergo a natural flow of solstices and that it's through those moments of solstice, that we are recreated and forged, which ultimately takes us to the next level in our evolution, making us better men for having undergone those solstices. I purposefully run toward those moments of solstice, because like men everywhere, I desire to be made into more, with the dawning of each new day. I was taught by the Senior Pastor of my church, Bishop Dr. T. Garrott Benjamin, Jr., that, *"Men are sent here only to serve. We are to serve firstly, God, secondly our families, thirdly our communities and then lastly, we are to serve ourselves, but only in ways that will guarantee that we become better servants to all"*. I am so very thankful for that teaching and I attempt to operate within that framework, daily.

As I selected the Poems that I would put into this section of my collection, I wanted to make sure that I chose the pieces that strongly affected my spirit, though I love every Poem in this component, I want to share that affect with all who will read this collection, but more especially, the men who read this collection. My need and desire for peace is indeed reflected in the entire collection, and what is of equal importance is that this section has allowed me to see, the maturity in myself and maturity promotes peace. I no longer write filled with that once driven sense of rebellion. I sought to find a reprieve through reflection, and I was able to do that. I next desired to start the healing process and I now know that, healing comes through redemption, and redemption is such a holistic healing.

The Redemption

An Erroneous Existence

He was born into a highly hostile existence
He grew up hard as a child, only desiring repentance
The biological man that dropped the seed
Left him alone and deserted
He courageously and brashly crept up to death's door
And with a heart filled with fire, he foolishly flirted
He was raised by a single mother who
Had to teach him to stand strong and tall
She told him, *"that it's because of your lineage that you mustn't fall"*
He would grow to be a man having a love for verse
And he possessed a gift for creating magic with didactic prose
If left alone to flourish he would have touched the sky, Lord knows
No one can judge him for the path that he chose
He was dealt a harsh reality by the hand of fate
Though he stood immovable to her destructive bumps and blows
Declared a militant by a world that didn't understand his soul
His was a desire to promote equality for the world
Though he didn't want to follow any societal controls
He would become a Cesar in the Pompeian like rap industry
His intelligence was vast, and his desire would flow endlessly
He became a star merely by the fact that God willed it
Although, because of the nature of Tupac's subject matter
Some in the world, said that he didn't really fit
He sought to educate a young nation
Only to be shot dead in the streets
His body was committed to the flame, and his soul was released
His spirit finally found the Gates of Heaven
For on that fateful day, Tupac Shakur had finally found peace

Angel's Wings

As morning dawned over the horizon
A shower of gold covered my eyes
For on this day my Godmother passed away
But in reality, and Angel died
As I held her in my arms, I felt her soul pass through mine
I believe that I saw the story of her life
Within that split second in time
My heart shattered into one thousand pieces
As I gazed up at the sky
Did she really have to go now Lord?
I asked humbly, wondering why
I had to say goodbye to her on that day
As she was given wings with which to reach the Heavens above
I was made a better man because of Sharon Birden
And the truest gift of her presence, was her ever sheltering love

At It Again

Here I am Lord, I'm at it again
Doing my thing, with this paper and pen
I've seen the faces in the dark coldness of night
Of my long buried peers
Victimized gems, who never saw their greatest years
I can't help but to recall the images
Of their twisted bodies and their melted minds
Either lost violently over drugs
Or jailed forever because of senseless crimes
What were they looking for? What were they hoping to find?
Bereaving mothers with increased intuition can see the signs of the times
No more blaming others for our community's current state
For now, we are oppressed from within
By this pandemic blanket of possessed self hate
A dreadful loathsome sin
As a nation we humbly beseech you Lord, as we fall to our knees
We are asking for divine intervention Father, please hear our pleads

A Wretch like Me

Once upon a time in my life, I found comfort in the darkness
Lacking honor and integrity, I often lied, stole and cheated
Was I acting out as others did in my lineage? Was a vicious cycle being repeated?
At times during rough tribulations, I would hear a voice saying
"Hold on my son, you won't be defeated"
But the battle with my duplicit self, was getting ugly, chaotic and heated
It was during these days that I lived as a miscreant
A transient on the highways of life, lost in the world's gutters
At times back then I could feel death so close to me
That I would be nearly driven mad, because I felt so smothered
I would sit and angrily ask God that if He could
Just let me know that I was alive, demanding that He'd send me a sign
Then hopelessness took over me, and His name I began to malign
I was walking the Earth as a zombie, living in complete sadness
And I stepped foolishly, to the edge of total madness
Then in the midst of chaos, I was overcome with a sense of tranquility
Guided by my once lost faith, I embraced His love with humility
Eager to be in His grace, I quickened my pace as I ran toward the gate
I suddenly became energized; finally, no longer did I have to wait
God had finally answered, and He blessed me with a life giving taste
I then fell to my knees, and tried to hold back the tears
I had been given providence, delivered from spiritual poverty and fear
Now I walk tall, I soar like an Eagle, strong and free
And eternally will I be thankful, for Him saving a wretch like me

Battle Shield

Prompted by a celestial order, to open my eyes to greet the Sun
A smile grows over my face, as I rejoice in this new day begun
As my spirit beckons for me to, I fall to my knees and pray
I'm searching for wisdom and understanding
As God molds my mind like clay
I once called out to Him, as I cried out for a sense of direction
Because I'm on that never ending quest
For the golden light of utopian perfection
God empowered my soul for the journey
So that it could take to the mountain high
He sent me a Heavenly chariot
So that I could soar across the sheltering sky

And during the times that the path gets rough and rocky
I'll take a moment to settle and rest
For He equipped me with all of the proper tools
He indoctrinated me to give life my best
I know that I'll have battles to fight
With both man and the elements
But I'll keep a soldier's composure
All battles I'll fight with elegance
And in the end my fortitude won't falter
Though I may at times trip and stumble
God gave me my marching orders
And they command that I remain both fierce and humble
So I'll keep on climbing upward, to the summit of the Earth's highest hill
Thanking God every step of the way, for Him giving me a heart like steel
He trained me for the war, and He equipped me with a Heavenly battle shield

Believe In You

Believe in you, when the days seem to be rough and at their heaviest
Believe in you when you're tired, but you can't rest to catch your breath
Believe in you when life gets harder, buckle up and stick out your chest
Believing in you is the one thing that will make you better than the rest
Believe in you when you feel alone, when it comes to the things that you choose
Believe in you when the race gets hard, and it appears that you may lose
Believe in you whenever you're tested, be the rock, tried and true
Believe in you when you're feeling lost, and to get back you don't have a clue
Believe in you when you imagine that you've walked ten miles
But only look down to find that you're still standing in the same spot
Believe in you when it seems that everyone, is out to get you for what you've got
Believe in you, when you're in the tightest jam, and your stomach is tied in knots
Believe in God, for in the end, He's the only one that can conquer the Devil's plots

Empyreal Visions

Crack filled pregnant mothers line the street corner
With the hopes of getting some of that government cheese
Their bodies are covered with dirt so heavy it's like chimney soot
And their hair is so matted and nappy, that it has become a nest for fleas
Their unborn babies are victimized before they draw their first breath
For their mothers are too wasted to pay attention to their prenatal needs

I visit friends who are locked up in the penitentiary
And all I see are poor whites, blacks and brown faces
Some committed a crime just to feed their families
But their deeds only succeeded to land them in the most hellish of places
As they are left alone to spend countless hours wasting away in a 6' by 9'
With only hopes and prayers to steady them, so that they don't lose their minds

I see silhouettes outlined in chalk which has become
So common place that it looks like near graffiti in our ghetto's streets
They are akin to the cave art, created by the original man
I yearn for the day when, we will be released from this Earthly pain
I have empyreal visions of God's goodness, and Heaven is the ultimate gain

Gates of Heaven

I pray that I will see those Gates of Heaven
And as I enter, let the Angels play their golden harps
Set me on the path toward wonderful
I want to feel the warmth of God's love in my heart
Let me do good deeds, for my fellow man
I want to leave a powerful legacy before I'm called to depart

Allow me to walk the road laden with diamonds
Only stopping to rest where the Angels dwell
Give me life eternal Lord
So that I can live under the empyreal spell
I'll become a soldier Angel
So that I can battle the legions of Hell
Peter and Michael will ready me for the journey
Teaching me the truths about Heaven and all of its wonderful tales

I pray to sit by the golden streams, to see their beauty so true and clear
I want to add to the nearby fountains, my purest and most innocent tears
Grant me the chance to see the familiar faces of those who were close and dear
Heaven grants me the strength, to never again live in fear
As I enter let the trumpets blow, for that's all I desire to hear
Let the Cherubs stand to their feet with pride
And then I'll know that I have arrived, when I hear St. Peter cheer

I'm Ready

I was created as my mother's middle child
And like a lion cub, my spirit was strong and wild
God blessed me with an incredible sense of desire
He encased the flame in the mightiest marble
In order to eternally protect its fire

He taught me to discern tomorrow
By looking into the future's eye
Showed me that one day alone I'd have to fly
He trained me and readied me
And prepped me for the battle
To slay all demons was my charge
Who'd turn me into chattel

Legion is my sworn enemy, he with his army strong
Set to fight the war of all wars
Atop the mountain, known as Megiddo
And in the end when I have departed this battle zone
I pray the gates of Heaven open wide
I'm ready, so please welcome my soul home

In the Eye of the Storm

The other day, a sixteen year old boy
Received a sentence of eighty years
His mama left the court room broken
Though she found no peace in her tears
Her once baby boy, would now be thrown into the land of man
So she stops for a second to kneel
Praying to God, that his soul won't be damned
Just months before, he committed a senseless murder
And he had now been judged and found guilty
One can only hope, that he won't grow old feeling cold and empty
His whole life is about to change, forcing him to decide
To become a barbarian in spirit, just to survive
He'll be used and abused as a throw about
If he doesn't become a victim to fratricide
This boy is now caught up, in the eye of the storm
Please Lord, pull him from the wreckage
And carry his spirit to that Heavenly place
Allowing him to find a sense of peace as he becomes airborne

Maze

I'm steadily dodging the bullets in my mind, created by my hellish past
It was because of my lust for mammon, I would have died just to have cash
I didn't want to work hard for it though; I felt a need to gain it fast
But You delivered me from those evils, you've taken me off of that beaten path
And I've learned to fear only You, I've grown wise to Heaven's wrath
A shirt and tie has replaced my all black hoodie, and my gang related rag
I've had nightmares of a violent death, a toe on my foot labeled with a white tag
I'm now on a mission for repentance, I'm on the quest to reconcile
My mission now is to save children, and to be everything the opposite of vile
I want to become viewed worthy, by supporting a cause that's worth wile
I now have a testimony; I've even felt my soul set ablaze
I thank you humbly Lord for leading me out of the darkness
Showing me the way out of the maze

Morose and Sullen

Never should you dwell in the depths of sadness
Walk with the confidence of knowing who made you
And be a victim no more to any worldly oppression
Find joy in this hour of jubilee, as you create a new sense of mission
Morose and sullen days will rob you of happiness
Just imagine all of the wonderful living that you're missing
Believe in your God given birthright of greatness
And let that guide you along life's path
And if you for one second question your purpose
God is always listening, so just ask
Majesty was yours at the moment of your conception
We are all imperfect beings following the example of
The one true being birthed from the womb of perfection
So open your heart, so that you can receive your blessings
You must always remember to stand tall
You must remember to walk with courage
In order to win it all

Old Scratch Enemy of Mankind

He is ever present forever lurking in the darkness
Trying his best to steal and corrupt souls
His presence is evident in the actions of
Child molesters, rapist and murders
These are people who were born of God
But tragically were turned and now
It's their spirits that he controls
He is Old Scratch the Deceiver
He is the serpent of old

He was once Heaven's most respected Angel
But was cast out as the eternal rebel
In my understanding, you can't
Acknowledge the presence of God
And not recognize the existence of the Devil
And though at times, it may appear that he's winning the battle
He leads an empty army, of minions of nothing more than chattel
And though it seem as though he's strong
Just know that he's not the strongest and he's running out of time
The end is drawing near for 'Old Scratch the Tricker', enemy of mankind

Ontogeny

Look closely at her walk, she steps with a majestic air
She's at the genesis of the first Egyptian lineage
Her spirit is as strong as the tallest oak tree, but touched with a noble flair
God didn't expunge her from Osiris' ribcage, God pulled her from his mind
She is the eternal symbol of beauty; her grace is strong and divine
And today's woman descended this source of greatness
Regality due her because of this royal bloodline

She is to be celebrated, and as men we should support her desires to fly
Like a rose in bloom she feeds off of her King's strength
As if it were the Sun, without it she'd simply wither away and die
God imbued her with character and value, as He empowers her so that she can shine
She'll ride on the back of winged horses, as her head touches the sky
God fuels the flame that burns within her
She's always inspired to spread her wings to take flight and rise
It's because of her ontogeny as a Queen, that she'll inherit Heaven's ultimate prize

Perfect Peace

I doubt that a day will pass, when we won't think of your face
Or feel the warmth of your grand spirit in our heart's special place
Today we sing in honor of you Grandfather
And as you continue to watch over us, we know that you'll hear it
On this fateful day, you were called to glory as you reached for the Heavens
I knew then that you wouldn't be far away, although God beckoned
I figured that I would lock you away deep inside in my heart
And I knew that I would again see you in my dreams
For on this day a man didn't die, but rather, an Angel received his wings

For so many of us, you were our foundational wellspring of stability
And you were the source of our family's strength
During the times that we sought refuge in our fragilities
Though you were small in stature
Giants were dwarfed by your character so grand
You lived your life an example of God fearing goodness
This made you the truest definition of a man

We give glory and honor to God, because you were Heaven sent
Eighty-three years in this place, a wonderful life well spent
Believe that your legacy remains, for it shines in the faces of your grandchildren
And it will eternally beat in the hearts of those yet to come
For we will pass on the legend of your greatness
Through the generations, so that they'll know all about the power of
The incredible lineage into which they were born
So sit back grandfather and listen to the golden harp as Gabriel plays
And watch as Peter and Michael leads the grand parade
I remember how sometimes you'd say, *"Oh Lord, please remember me"*
Well, He did grandfather, and now you can rest in perfect peace

Polished With Fire and Desire

His hands are carved out of black marble, and polished with fire and desire
Imported from North Africa, he was touted as the universe's greatest sire
He has been defined as a truly remarkable King
He has passed on to his progeny the gift of his most sensational dreams
He was guided by the spirits of his ancestors, to walk across moonbeams
And the tears that flow from his eyes are as pure as cool running streams
His regality is uncompromised, for he is the descendent of Saharan Kings

You black man, the progenitor to Adam, Moses and Abraham
You who flowed from within the celestial loins of Ham and Shem
You have granted me the gift of character
It's you who makes me who I am
I am filled with an eternal source of confidence
For my life goes according to God's plan
And though we are now lost, we must again look to you, to show us the way
We must remember the greatness of who we are
Especially in the midst of this chaos that we face everyday
We must stand and turn, to run toward deliverance's blinding light
We are as powerful as the darkened skies
That shelters us in the celestial dawning of night

Realization

I saw this young man, stepping with his cool, *"I'm the man walk"*
With his hat leaning to the side of his head
Talking to a young lady with some of that old pimp talk
You would have never have known that he graduated Cum Laude
By the designs that he had trying to get close to her body
I would see this young man from time to time
And each time I did, I'd see that he would be wearing a smile
Then one day it dawned on me, I wanted to sit and study his style
I noticed how he would greet each lady he'd pass with a, *"how do you do?"*
I later asked about that, and he replied
"My grandfather said to always admonish a lady
And when you do it, be authentic and true"
Then I asked, what's the inspiration that makes you smile that way?
He said, *"Because I'm thankful to the Lord, for giving me another day"*
"And the inspiration is passed to me, through warm Sun rays"

Well, the last time I saw him, I had one more question for him
One that I was sure would make him have to sit and postulate
I felt comfortable asking this question because of how familiar we'd become
I asked, what is the single greatest thing you've ever done?
He stared at me for a second, and then he looked toward the sky
He stood there quietly for a moment, and then he sighed
He then looked at me, and cracked a smile as he replied
"I learned to thank God for the Son He gave that died"
"And it was then my friend that I began to feel alive"
It was at that moment of realization that I truly began to see
That this man was no stranger, but rather, this man was me

The Ultimate Progenitor

I was born an heir to the ascended Lamb
For I was trained to carry the weight of the world
I've been a student to the great teacher Gamaliel
I have survived my pilgrimage through the battle lands
I was schooled to the secrets of war
By the scripted notes created by the Chinese philosopher Sun
I have ridden on the backs of mighty winged Eagles
In order to touch the Sun with each new day begun

I have the strongest desire to be the best that I can be
For they once said that I was a symbol without substance
Whose cup had runneth empty
I have seen the power of Jehovah, and that makes me walk with a meek air
I am the dichotomized mix of humility and intensity
Both touched with a rebellious flair
It's because of my knowledge of who made me
That I know that I will one day touch the sky
I will leap carefree from the cliff of life
And like the mighty Phoenix, spread my wings to fly
And in the end when my work is complete
I'll be granted providence, as I walk through Heaven's door
I have a date with my empyreal destiny see
For I am the ultimate progenitor

Today

Today I awake to be all that I can
I promise to stay motivated
In order to follow through with the plan
To always remain modestly humble and
To reach out my hands to my fellow man
Be the anchor for him, when no more he can stand

Today I awake to be all that I can be
To weather the storm on land or sea
To continue the fight until there is total equality
To be the beacon for all, who strive to be free

Today I awake as a child of God
To help spread the news of Heaven's golden rod
To continue to pray, nurturing the power within
To help develop a plan for the world, that will heal and mend

Today I've been blessed to breathe again
To follow in the footsteps of Jesus, the Son of Man
Today I stare out across the golden sky
I smile at the sun, and spread my wings to fly

Tomorrow Anew

Dear God, tonight I pray to start tomorrow anew
I'm beseeching You for Your guidance on the things that I choose
I know that You'll walk with me, even in the pit of my darkest day
I want to be the shinning example, of Your blinding goodness in every way
To affect change around the world positively, is all I pray

Let me energize the world, with the same sovereignty of the Sun
Let me link the bonds of men, into the singular power of one
Let me step into the jungle, ever ready to strive
I'll walk with an air of dominion, because I'm feeling so alive
Let me destroy all negative energy and any destructive mood
Dear God, tonight I pray to start tomorrow anew

Too Tired To Fall

During some of the roughest times in my life
I have felt so lost, while searching for me
Desiring strength for my spirit, praying to be free
Give me direction, as I quest for perfection
And equip me with an empyreal battle shield for my protection
Grant me endurance so that I don't fall before I complete my task
When my time has come, take my spirit home, is all that I ask
Sometimes I see the world through the eyes of a child
Is my heart too strong, or is my spirit too wild?
A misunderstood soul, is what I've grown to be
Release me now Lord, please take all of me

If I'm to climb the mountain, please empower me for the ride
You know my soul Father, my dreams I cannot hide
Grant me the understanding, to do away with my foolish pride
Give me endurance for the journey; it's my time to rise
And all the while during this climb
Grant me an intense focus, and please free my mind
I'll keep my head looking upward, for I know that I must stand tall
I'm a soldier who's too strong to be broken
And I am much too tired to fall